THE STORY OF THE OLYMPICS

Other books by Richard Brassey

Ghosts! The Ultimate Guide for Ghost Hunters

Faster, Further, Higher, Deeper

The Story of London

The Story of Scotland

Nessie the Loch Ness Monster

Greyfriars Bobby

THE STORY OF THE OLYMPICS

THE WACKY FACTS ABOUT THE OLYMPICS AND OLYMPIC CHAMPIONS DOWN THE CENTURIES!

RICHARD BRASSEY

Orion
Children's Books

First published in Great Britain in 2011 by Orion Children's Books
This edition published in Great Britain in 2016 by Hodder and Stoughton

1 3 5 7 9 10 8 6 4 2

Text and illustrations copyright © Richard Brassey 2011, 2016

The right of Richard Brassey to be identified as the author and illustrator of this work has been asserted.

A CIP catalogue record for this book is available from the British Library.

ISBN 978 1 5101 0138 8

Printed and bound in China.

The paper and board used in this book are from well-managed forests
and other responsible sources.

Orion Children's Books
An imprint of Hachette Children's Group
Part of Hodder & Stoughton
Carmelite House
50 Victoria Embankment London EC4Y 0DZ
An Hachette UK Company

www.hachette.co.uk
www.hachettechildrens.co.uk

"Sport has the power to change the world.
It has the power to unite in a way that little else does.
It speaks to youth in a language they understand.
Sport can create hope where once there was only
despair. It is more powerful than governments in
breaking down racial barriers. It laughs in
the face of all types of discrimination."

Nelson Mandela

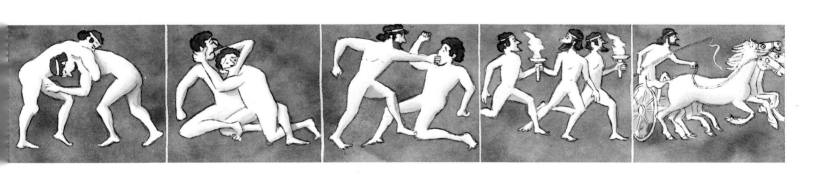

BC	776	720	560	490	456

START OF 1ST OLYMPIAD

FIRST GAMES AT OLYMPIA | ATHLETES TAKE OFF THEIR SHORTS | FIRST STADIUM BUILT | PHEIDIPPIDES' MARATHON RUN | TEMPLE OF ZEUS COMPLETED

How old are you?

Two and a half Olympiads.

THE OLYMPIAD AND THE OLYMPIC TRUCE

In ancient times the land of Greece was made up of many small kingdoms, which constantly fought among themselves. But every four years they agreed to put aside their differences and send their best athletes to compete with each other in games held at a place named Olympia. The four-year period between the start of one games and the next became known as an Olympiad. It was even used to measure time.

The games at Olympia were not just a sporting event. They were also a religious festival dedicated to Zeus, the king of the Greek gods. After 293 Olympiads, Christianity became the state religion of Rome and the Emperor put a stop to the Games.

Let's stop the war for a bit and run some races instead.

OK

These Games are unchristian.

668TH OLYMPIAD

1600	1766	1896	1900	1916

FIRST COTSWOLD OLIMPICKS | REDISCOVERY OF ANCIENT OLYMPIA | FIRST GAMES OF THE MODERN ERA | FIRST WOMEN COMPETE | WORLD WAR ONE · NO GAMES

146 — ROMANS ARRIVE AND TAKE OVER THE GAMES

AD 67 — EMPEROR NERO COMPETES IN CHARIOT

393 — ROMAN EMPEROR THEODOSIUS BANS THE GAMES AS PAGAN CULT.

426 — TEMPLE OF ZEUS BURNT TO THE GROUND.

It's more important in life to compete than to triumph. To have fought well is the main thing, not to have won.

Pierre de Coubertin

THE OLYMPIC IDEAL

When Baron Pierre de Coubertin restarted the Olympic Games just over a hundred years ago, he hoped the meeting of athletes from all over the world would lead to peace and better understanding between nations. He also hoped that the athletes would take part for the joy of sport and not just for money or fame.

Today athletes from almost every nation compete to be the best in their chosen sport. It doesn't matter what country they come from. People in every part of the world can take pleasure in watching them do the best they can.

1924 — FIRST WINTER OLYMPICS

1928 — FIRST WOMEN'S TRACK & FIELD EVENTS

1936 — FIRST TORCH RELAY FROM OLYMPIA

1940/44 — WORLD WAR TWO · NO GAMES

1960 FIRST PARALYMPICS
1968 FIRST SPECIAL OLYMPICS
2010 FIRST YOUTH OLYMPICS

THE OLYMPIC GAMES OF ANCIENT GREECE

DID HERACLES START THE OLYMPICS?

The Greek myths tell us how mighty Heracles cleaned the stinky Augean stables by damming the river Alpheus so it flowed through them. Afterwards he cleared all the rocks from the plain beside the river, known as the Altis, and held the first Olympic Games there in honour of his father, Zeus.

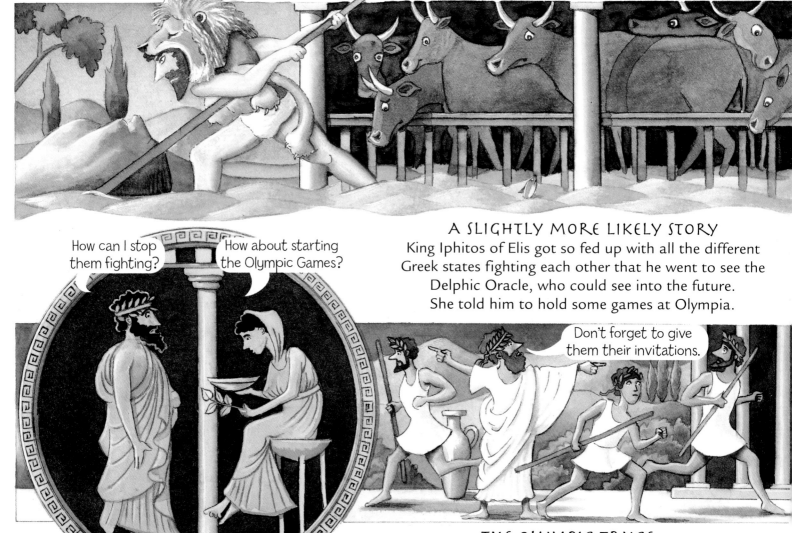

A SLIGHTLY MORE LIKELY STORY

King Iphitos of Elis got so fed up with all the different Greek states fighting each other that he went to see the Delphic Oracle, who could see into the future. She told him to hold some games at Olympia.

THE OLYMPIC TRUCE

Iphitos sent heralds to every state to announce a truce so athletes and spectators could travel to the Games without fear of attack.

THE OLYMPIC PROCESSION

The Games were to be held every four years after the harvest. The first took place in 776 BC. Two days before they began, officials, athletes and trainers set out on the two-day walk from Elis to Olympia.

In the 720BC Olympics, Orsippos' shorts fell down and tripped him up during a race.

To stop this happening again, the judges told the athletes to take their shorts off.

And, for the next thousand years, Olympic competitors wore no clothes at all.

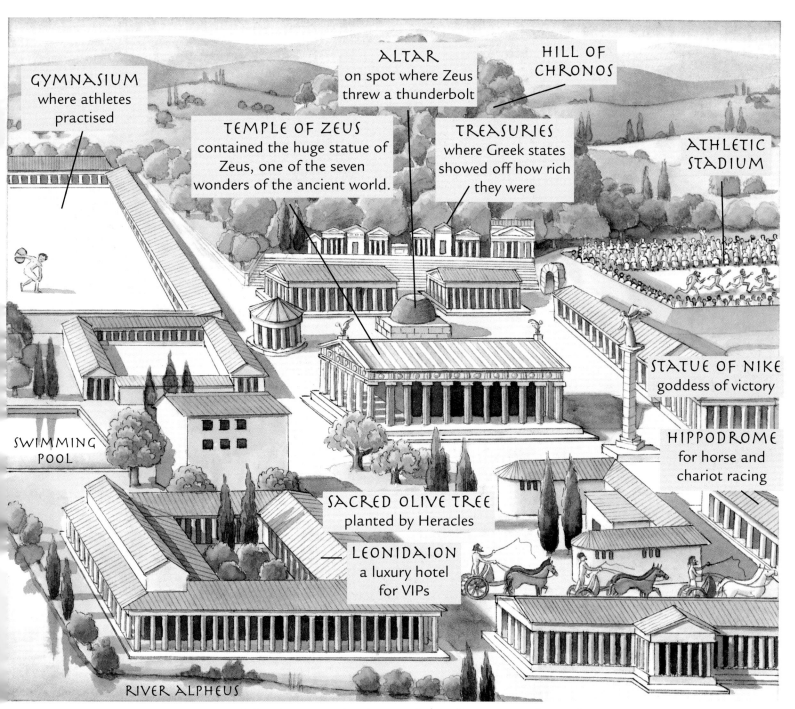

GYMNASIUM
where athletes practised

ALTAR
on spot where Zeus threw a thunderbolt

HILL OF CHRONOS

TEMPLE OF ZEUS
contained the huge statue of Zeus, one of the seven wonders of the ancient world.

TREASURIES
where Greek states showed off how rich they were

ATHLETIC STADIUM

SWIMMING POOL

STATUE OF NIKE
goddess of victory

HIPPODROME
for horse and chariot racing

SACRED OLIVE TREE
planted by Heracles

LEONIDAION
a luxury hotel for VIPs

RIVER ALPHEUS

THE SITE OF THE ORIGINAL OLYMPIC GAMES
In time the sports complex spread over the Altis plain at Olympia. The Games were an important religious festival dedicated to the god Zeus. The Greek states competed to build temples and other fine buildings.

SHORT FOOT RACE LONG FOOT RACE DISCUS JAVELIN LONG JUMP

PROGRAMME OF ANCIENT OLYMPICS

DAY 1 — I will obey the rules.

THE OLYMPIC OATH

DAY 2

FULL-MOON FEASTING

DAY 3

SACRIFICE TO ZEUS

A boar was sacrificed and athletes and judges took an oath. If they broke it they could be whipped.

The second night of the festival always coincided with the full moon when a great feast was held.

A hundred oxen were sacrificed on the altar of Zeus. The pile of ash was left to grow higher every year.

DAY 4

THE RACE IN ARMOUR

DAY 5

THE PRIZEGIVING

On the last day the winners processed to the Temple of Zeus to be crowned with leaves from the sacred olive grove. There were no prizes but winners were often well rewarded by their home state. Second and third place didn't even get medals . . . as they do today.

KLUTZ ALERT - CHARMOS

Keep going, Charmos!

Charmos was way behind the other five in his race. A friend ran beside him to cheer him on. Charmos couldn't even keep up with him. He finished seventh!

This house is your reward.

We made a statue of you.

1,000 jars of olive oil. It's a gift.

| WRESTLING | PANKRATION | BOXING | RELAY | CHARIOT RACE |

FIVE TIMES WRESTLING CHAMPION

MILO OF CROTON
Between 536 and 520BC, Milo won he wrestling at five successive Games. Many stories were told of his mighty strength. He once carried a cow around the Altis on his shoulders all day. Then he ate it whole for dinner.

TWELVE TIMES CHAMPION OF THE ANCIENT GAMES

LEONIDAS OF RHODES
Leonidas won all three different foot-races at four Olympics in a row from 164 to 156BC. He was not only the greatest sprinter but he also won the Race in Armour, which needed strength and endurance.

STRONGEST PANKRATIST CHAMPION EVER

POLYDAMAS OF SKOTOUSSA
Pankration was a free-for-all mix of wrestling and boxing. In 408 BC Polydamas, the greatest pankratist ever, was crowned with laurels from the sacred olive grove (see page 9). It's said he was so strong that he once strangled a lion with his bare hands.

THE END OF THE ANCIENT GAMES
The ancient Games lasted a thousand years until Theodosius, a Christian Emperor of Rome, banned them. In time earthquakes made the temples tumble and the ruins disappeared beneath mud when the rivers changed course.

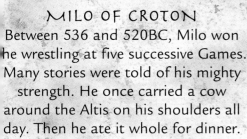

KLUTZ ALERT – NERO
The Emperor Nero entered the two-horse chariot race with ten horses. He fell off and never finished. The judges still declared him winner.

THE MODERN OLYMPICS

After the ancient Games ended, nothing much happened Olympics-wise for a thousand years. Then in 1600 some 'Olimpicks' were held in England, in the Cotswolds. The main events were horseracing, hunting and shin-kicking. Over the years occasional so-called 'Olympics' took place in other countries too.

Also in England, Dr Penny Brookes, from Much Wenlock, founded an 'Olympian Society'. In 1890 he had a French visitor, Baron Pierre de Coubert

Sports-mad Pierre was in despair at the laziness of French schoolboys. He liked the way pupils at English public schools were made to play field sports.

Pierre wanted everybody to be interested in sport. His brainwave came when he saw a model of the ancient site at Olympia. He invited sportsmen from 80 countries to an international conference. They all agreed to revive the Olympic Games in Athens in two years time, with Pierre in charge.

ATHENS

1896

Two hundred and forty-five athletes from fourteen nations competed in an ancient marble stadium, specially restored for the occasion. Champions were awarded silver medals and crowns of laurel leaves. The first event was a heat of the 100 metre dash, won by Francis Lane, USA. Several tourists who happened to be in Athens joined in.

FIRST CHAMPION OF THE MODERN ERA

James Connolly

James, from Boston, USA, nearly didn't make it to Athens when his wallet was stolen in Naples on the way. He won the very first gold medal on the first day for the Hop, Hop and Jump.

PARIS

1900

The second Olympiad in Paris went on for six whole months! For the first time nineteen of the 1,225 competing athletes were women ... though only in the croquet, tennis and golf.

YOUNGEST EVER MEDAL WINNER

See you!

Thanks

Dutch rowers Brandt and Klein decided their adult cox was too heavy. Instead they used a seven-year-old boy from the crowd. He ran off after the final, never to be seen again. Rowing and swimming took place on the Seine. The current was so strong that some of the records set were not beaten for years.

ST LOUIS

1904

Yet another American winner!

For the first time gold, silver and bronze medals were awarded. The US government had promised a ship to collect athletes from Europe but never sent it, so nearly all the athletes were American.

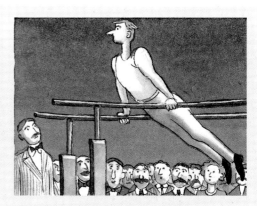

American gymnast George Eyser won six medals even though he had a wooden leg. He'd lost his left leg when he was run over by a train.

THE MARATHON

Amazingly, today's great closing event was never a part of the Ancient Games.

The legend goes that when the Persian army landed at Marathon in 490 BC an Athenian named Pheidippides ran 150 miles to Sparta to get help. He then ran back to Marathon to find the Athenians had already beaten the Persians, so he raced to Athens and just managed to gasp news of the victory before croaking.

It's 25 miles from Marathon to Athens. Pierre and the others thought it would be great to end the 1896 Games with a race over that distance.

Edwin Flack of Australia was a great athlete but he failed to finish the first Marathon in Athens despite being accompanied by a butler on a bicycle.

FIRST MARATHON CHAMPION

Spiridon Louis

Spiridon was a water-carrier from Athens. The home crowd were ecstatic when he entered the stadium in first place. The king said he could have any prize he wanted. He asked for a new water cart. To 'do a Louis' in Greek still means to run very fast.

KLUTZ ALERT!

The 54-year marathon

Shizo Kanaguri seemed to vanish during the 1912 race. In fact he'd fallen asleep beside the road. In 1966 he returned to Stockholm to finish the course.

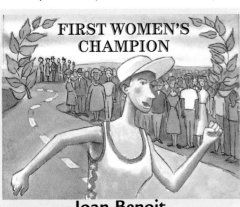

FIRST WOMEN'S CHAMPION

Joan Benoit

The first women's marathon was not introduced until 1984! It was won by Joan, from Maine, USA, wearing her trademark painter's hat.

In 2004 the race was once again run from Marathon to Athens. It was sadly spoilt when a spectator pushed the leader, de Lima of Brazil, off the course.

THE WACKY MARATHON

With competitors nearly dying from exhaustion, taking shortcuts and disappearing, the early marathons often seem more like the Wacky Races than an Olympic event. But none was wackier than the St Louis Marathon of 1904.

3. Two judges are hurt when their car crashes off the road.

2. It's a very hot day. Horsemen gallop ahead raising so much dust that everybody starts choking. Neither the runners nor the cars following can see where they're going.

START

Juicy apples. I'm starving.

. At the start Cuban postman Felix Carvajal is wearing his smartest shirt, trousers and polished shoes. A few snips from some cissors quickly turn his trousers into shorts.

4. South African Len Tau is chased miles off course by a large yellow dog.

It was only a joke.

FINISH

11. When Fred runs into the stadium, the crowds cheer. He's about to be given the gold medal when his cheating is revealed. Tom is declared champion although he's had to go straight to hospital. Only half the runners finish. Felix groans in at fourth. Len arrives ninth, having lost the dog.

5. Felix, in third place, stops to pick apples.

6. Fred Lotz of New York, USA gets cramps. He climbs into his trainer's car to drive back to the stadium.

This'll pep you up!

Ow! Ow! My stomach aches.

7. Felix's apples were unripe!

Thanks for the lift.

10. Tom Hicks, stumbling along in a poisoned daze, is amazed when Fred races by, fresh as a daisy.

8. Thomas Hicks of Boston, USA is exhausted. His trainer gives him strychnine poison . . . to give him energy!

9. Fred's trainer's car breaks down. Fred decides to jog the last couple of miles back to the stadium.

LONDON

1908

THE FIRST OPENING PARADE

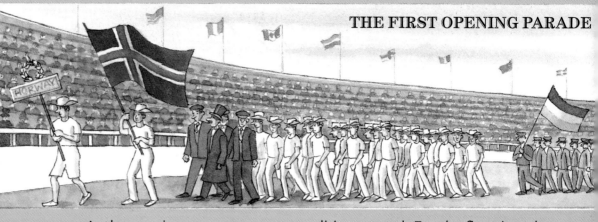

At the opening ceremony a new tradition started. For the first time the teams marched into the stadium behind their national flags. The White City Stadium had been specially built in just ten months. With its racetrack, cycle track, swimming pool etc., it set the standard for all future Olympic venues.

10 GOLD MEGA CHAMPION

Ray Ewry

Ray, from Indiana, USA, was an invalid as a boy because he had polio but went on to become a high-jumper. With two golds in London and eight from previous games, he set a record unequalled for a century.

THE TUG-OF-WAR

Those boots are illegal!

The 1908 US tuggers withdrew in a sulk saying the British police team had cheated by putting spikes on their boots. This event ended after 1920.

OLDEST EVER GOLD (and silver) MEDALLIST

Oscar Schwan was sixty when he won gold for the curiously named Running Deer Shooting. He was still at it in 1920 winning a silver medal aged seventy-two

STOCKHOLM

1912

How many more hours?

One semi-final of the Greco-Roman wrestling lasted nearly twelve hours, making it the longest match ever. The winner, Martin Klein of Estonia, was far too tired to compete in the final.

I think this one might be the winner.

When there was still no winner in the Light Heavyweight final after nine hour the judges gave both contestants a silve medal. Either one might be the winne

ANTWERP

1920

We swear we will take part in the Olympic Games in a spirit of chivalry, for the honour of our country and for the glory of sport.

Antwerp saw the introduction of the Olympic Flag and the Athlete's Oath. The fencing Nadi brothers of Italy dominated the Games. Nedo won five golds while Aldo won three golds and one silver.

PARIS

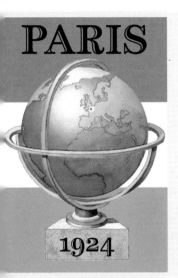

1924

'Swifter, Higher, Stronger' — the Olympic motto, first used in Paris, was Pierre's idea.

THE FIRST CLOSING CEREMONY

In a new ceremony to close the Games, the Olympic flag and the flags of France, as host, and Holland, as next host, were hoisted side by side. This was to be Pierre's last Olympiad as President of the IOC.

THE FLYING FINN

Paavo Nurmi

Finnish runner Paavo won 3 golds at Antwerp, 5 in Paris and 1 in Amsterdam. If the IOC hadn't banned him in 1932, claiming he had turned professional, he might have been the greatest champion of all time.

Now we'll see who's the real winner.

After the Games ended, two real life fencing duels were fought between Italian and Hungarian competitors in an argument over scores.

THE FIRST BLACK CHAMPION

Running Long Jumper William Dehart Hubbard of Indiana, USA became the first black athlete to win a gold medal at an Olympiad.

AAH-EEE-Aah-eee-aah!

US swimmer Johnny Weissmuller won three gold medals. He went on to be world famous as Tarzan in six Hollywood movies.

AMSTERDAM
1928

Women's athletics finally introduced.

Swimming events for women had been going since 1912. In the 1928 breaststroke final, Hilde Schrader of Germany swam so fast that her swimsuit straps snapped. She was too shy to get out of the pool.

The longest of the new track events for women was the 800 metres. When several of the competitors lay down after the finish to get their breath back, the newspapers made up stories of how they'd collapsed during the race. This led to all future women's track events over 200 metres being banned.

LOS ANGELES
1932

The games were held in the LA Coliseum, the largest stadium in the world. One lonely athlete represented China. Sprinter Liu Chang Chun didn't win any medals but he did make history.

MIGHT'VE-BEEN WHO CAME BACK FROM THE DEAD

Betty Robinson

Betty of Chicago, USA won the first women's 100 metre gold in 1928. She missed the 1932 games because for seven months she'd been in a coma after a plane crash! But she recovered and came back to win a gold in the 1936 relay.

GREATEST ALL-ROUND MIGHT'VE-BEEN

Mildred 'Babe' Didrikson

Babe, from Texas, USA, was a champion at almost every sport. She broke records in javelin, hurdles, high-jump and baseball throw at the 1932 Amateur Championships. But in the Olympics she was only allowed to enter three events. She won two golds and a silver. Who knows how many more she might have won! Instead she turned pro at golf and won ten major championships.

WOMEN IN THE OLYMPICS

There were no female competitors in the ancient Games. Even in the modern era,
it took a long time before women were allowed to compete in more than a handful of events.

Women were not even allowed to attend the ancient Games at Olympia. Any caught sneaking in were taken to a nearby mountain and thrown off.

Rich women could enter chariot teams, as owners. The rest had to make do with the separate Games of Hera, consisting of just one foot race.

A Greek woman, Stamata Revithi, was so fed up at not being allowed to compete in the Marathon of 1896 that she ran the course by herself next day.

While visiting Paris in the summer of 1900 some women took part in sports such as ballooning, croquet and golf, not realising they were competing in the Games. Margaret Abbott of Chicago, USA won a golf tournament. She died in 1955 never knowing she'd been the first American woman to win gold.

FIRST EVER WOMEN'S CHAMPION

Charlotte Cooper
UK tennis player – became first ever female gold in 1900.

MEN AND WOMEN COMPETE DIRECTLY

In sailing there have been mixed events since 1908 when Frances Rivett-Carnac, UK, became the first female gold crew-member.

In 1952 the equestrian events were opened to women and are today the only sport in which men and women compete one on one.

After 1928, the 800 metres for women was not run again until 1964! There was not even a female member of the IOC until 1984.

BERLIN

1936

First time the torch was carried from Olympia

Try it this way.

Thanks, Lutz.

DE COUBERTIN MEDAL
LUTZ LONG *for* sportsmanship

The Nazis didn't allow any 'non-Aryan' Germans to compete. But not all Germans were racist. Lutz Long even advised Jesse Owens on his long-jump technique and, as a result, Jesse beat him.

The Games were televised for the first time. Unfortunately hardly anybody in those days had a TV set to watch them on.

US diver Marjorie Gestring (aged 13) became the youngest ever to win gold, Danish swimmer Inge Sorensen (aged 12) bronze.

THE MISSING OLYMPICS
The next Olympiad had been scheduled for Tokyo in 1940 but was cancelled when World War Two broke out. There were no more games until 1948.

LONDON

1948

He's too heavy.

How about shaving all his hair off?

Although quite chaotic — the scales used to weigh the boxers were inaccurate and the judges lost count when Emil Zátopek lapped nearly all his competitors — the 1948 Games cheered the world up after the war. See page 28 for more.

THE BERLIN CHAMPION

Jesse Owens
Jesse, from Cleveland USA, won four golds in sprint, long jump and relay. This really annoyed Adolf Hitler, who believed Europeans were better at everything than people of African descent. Afterwards Jesse turned pro, so, sadly, he was banned from ever competing in the Olympics again.

THE FLYING HOUSEWIFE

Fanny Blankers-Koen
Because of the war, this Dutch mother of two missed any chance for Olympic medals until 1948 when she won four golds — in sprinting, hurdling and relay. She was a brilliant all-rounder and might have won medals in high and long jump too if she'd been allowed to enter more events.

HELSINKI

1952

First time a team from the USSR competed.

KLUTZ ALERT!

"You're not allowed to run."

"Try and catch us then."

Fritz Schwab and Bruno Junk

The race-walking rules stated that all disqualifications must be handed out during the race. In the final, Fritz (Switzerland) and Bruno (USSR) ran to the finish line before the judges could catch them.

THE CZECH LOCOMOTIVE

CH ... CHOO ... CHOO ... CHOO

DE COUBERTIN MEDAL EMIL ZÁPOTEK for sportsmanship

Emil Zátopek

Emil got his nickname from the wheezing sound he made as he ran. He trained after work, at night in all weathers, wearing army boots. He not only won gold and broke the world records in the 5,000 and 10,000 in Helsinki but also in the Marathon, which he'd never run before. He became a hero among the Czech people but was disgraced by the government for supporting democracy.

MELBOURNE

1956

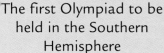

The first Olympiad to be held in the Southern Hemisphere

18-year-old Vyacheslav Ivanov (USSR) won his first of three golds for single sculls. He was so excited he threw it in the air but forgot to catch it. The medal disappeared to the bottom of the lake.

ROME

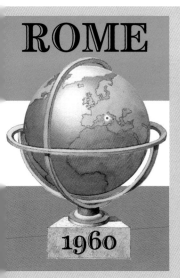

1960

Despite running barefoot and nearly colliding with a scooter, Abebe Bikila won the Marathon. Nobody expected an African to win. The band didn't even know the Ethiopian national anthem.

18-year-old boxer Cassius Clay from Kentucky, USA won light heavyweight gold. He changed his name in 1964... to Mohammed Ali.

TOKYO

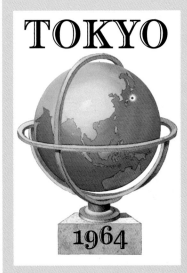

1964

First Olympiad in Asia

Several athletes have met and fallen in love at the Games. Bulgarian long-jumper Diana Yorgova and gymnast Nikolai Prodanov were the first to actually tie the knot in the Olympic Village.

Larisa Latynina

Gymnast Larissa from Kherson, Ukraine won four golds in Melbourne, three in Rome and finally two in Tokyo, making her one of the select few athletes — and the only woman — ever to win nine. After she retired she became coach to the Soviet team and organised the gymnastics competition in the 1980 Moscow Olympics.

MEXICO CITY

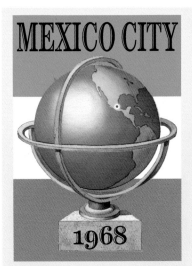

1968

The highest altitude games ever. Lack of oxygen was a problem for some athletes.

The air's so thin I can hardly breathe.

They're calling it 'The Fosbury Flop'.

Dick Fosbury of Oregon, USA amazed the judges with his back-down high-jump technique. They were afraid he might break his back but he won gold and other jumpers were soon copying it.

MUNICH

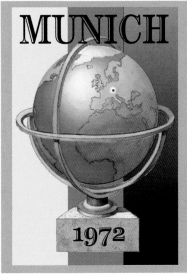

1972

Munich will always be remembered for an attack by Palestinian terrorists, which led to the death of eleven Israeli athletes.

That's our race!

Rey Robinson and Eddie Hart (USA) were sitting in the Village when they saw the sprint heats they were meant to be in on TV. Their team coach had forgotten to tell them the time had been changed.

Mark Spitz

Mark, from Sacramento, USA, was a schools swimming champion. He boasted he'd win six golds in Mexico City but only won two. To make up he won seven in Munich, the most ever in a single Games up till then. Afterwards, although only 22, he retired from swimming. He'd planned to be a dentist but went into business instead.

POLITICS AND THE OLYMPICS
Politics have often interfered in the games and probably always will.

In 365 BC the King of Elis lost control of Olympia. The following year a battle for its possession raged during the actual Games.

There's blood in the water.

In 1956, after the USSR had invaded Hungary, a water polo match between their two teams turned into an all-out fight.

In 1968 Tommie Smith and John Carlos, who won medals in the 200 metres, protested against racism in the USA and South Africa.

In 1980 sixty-five nations refused to send teams to Moscow after the USSR invaded Afghanistan. Tit for tat, the USSR stayed at home in 1984.

TRAINING TO BE AN OLYMPIC ATHLETE

Ow! Ow! I am trying.

Do you think she's old enough to start training for the Olympics?

Only another eight hours and you'll be done for the day.

Ancient Greek coaches made athletes eat special diets, such as dried figs and cheese, and beat them if they didn't try hard enough.

Some of today's champions began training in their sport as young as two or three years old, but that doesn't mean you can't start later.

Often athletes become coaches themselves after they retire. They know just how many hours training it takes to become a champion.

MONTREAL

1976

Only host country to win no gold medals

She only scored one!

The scoreboard doesn't go up to ten.

Nadia Comaneci (Romania) took up gymnastics in kindergarten. In Montreal, aged 14, she was the first gymnast to score a ten and will always be youngest ever to win gold as competitors must now be sixteen.

Sawao Kato

Sawao, from Nigata, Japan, won the first three of his eight golds in Mexico City and the last two in Montreal. This makes him the most successful male Olympic gymnast of all time.

MOSCOW

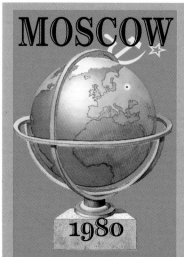

1980

The USA and sixty-four other countries did not send teams (see POLITICS page 23)

Steve won the 800 metres.

Seb won the 1,500.

Middle distance UK runners Sebastian Coe and Steve Ovett beat each other in the races they were expected to win. Lord Coe went on to take charge of organising London 2012.

NOT A KLUTZ
Paralysed By Fear

You will run as though your life depends on it ... which it does!

Dieudonné Lamothe

Why was Dieudonné's 5000 metres in Montreal the slowest ever? Why did he trail in last in the Moscow Marathon? He explained years later. Baby Doc, the dictator of Haiti, had threatened him with death if he didn't finish. Instead of making him run faster, he was paralysed with fear. After Doc's overthrow, Dieudonné did much better, coming 20th in Seoul.

LOS ANGELES

1984

Seventeen-year-old South African Zola Budd hero-worshipped world record holder Mary Decker (USA). But when she ran against Mary in the 3000 metre final, she accidentally tripped her.

SPORTSMAN OF THE CENTURY

Carl Lewis

In 1999 the IOC voted US sprinter Carl Lewis of Birmingham, Alabama, the twentieth century's greatest athlete. He won nine Olympic golds between 1984 and 1996, dominating the 100 metres, 200 metres and the long jump.

SEOUL

1988

The second games to be held in Asia

Korean Sohn Kee-Chung had annoyed Hitler as much as Jesse Owens had by winning the Berlin Marathon in 1936. Fifty-two years later, he carried the torch into the stadium in Seoul.

Christa Luding (Germany) won medals in both summer and winter Games of 1988 ... impossible now as these events are held two years apart.

EIGHT GOLDS SWIMMER

Matt Biondi

Matt, from California, USA, won a total of eight golds. He won five in Seoul, and broke four world records.

BARCELONA

1992

1992 saw big changes to some major medal-winning countries. The USSR was now split into fifteen separate nations while East and West Germany had been reunited.

Why's he not on video between start and finish?

KLUTZ ALERT!

Apolinario Gomez? My foot! That's Polin.

Polin Belisle

How did he get there?

No sign of him after mile one.

Despite doing mysteriously well in other Marathons, Polin came last in Seoul. Team Belize dropped him. Then in Barcelona his former teammates recognized a new Honduran runner. Even after Honduras dumped him, he still cheekily crashed the start ... and then he vanished.

ATLANTA

1996

Halfway through the Atlanta Games — one hundred years after the first modern Olympiad — a terrorist bomb exploded, killing one person and injuring over a hundred others. It was decided to continue the Games.

Hey! We forgot Kerri.

The hero of the games was 19-year-old gymnast Kerri Strug of Arizona, USA who vaulted with a badly sprained ankle to ensure her team won. She had to be carried onto the podium for the prize-giving and nearly got left behind when it was over.

SYDNEY

2000

This was only the second Olympiad to be held in the Southern hemisphere

You can do it.

KLUTZ ALERT! Eric the Eel

Go Eric!

My muscles are aching.

Eric Moussambani
Eric of Equatorial Guinea had only just learnt to swim in a small hotel pool. His time was the slowest ever for the 100 metres, twice that of any of the other competitors ... but his personal best!

LONGEST SERVING CHAMPION

Birgit Fischer
Kayaker Birgit of Brandenburg, Germany, won her first gold at Moscow in 1980 and her eighth twenty-four years later in Athens. With four silver medals as well, she is the second highest woman medal winner.

ATHENS

2004

The Olympic flame, first lit by the rays of the sun at a ceremony in ancient Olympia, was carried all around the world before returning to ignite the cauldron above the stadium in Athens.

BEIJING
2008

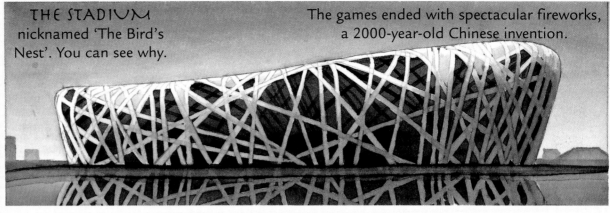

THE STADIUM nicknamed 'The Bird's Nest'. You can see why.

The games ended with spectacular fireworks, a 2000-year-old Chinese invention.

The biggest Games to date, with eleven thousand athletes from 204 countries. Huge amounts were spent on preparations, including the world's fastest train, biggest air terminal and the huge National Stadium. The opening ceremony had fifteen thousand performers. It began at 8.08 on the eighth day of the eighth month ... Eight is a very lucky number in China.

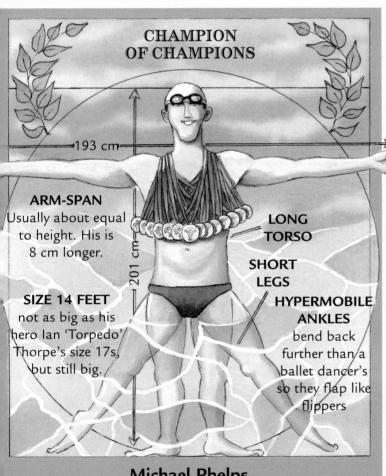

CHAMPION OF CHAMPIONS

←193 cm→

201 cm

ARM-SPAN
Usually about equal to height. His is 8 cm longer.

SIZE 14 FEET
not as big as his hero Ian 'Torpedo' Thorpe's size 17s, but still big.

LONG TORSO

SHORT LEGS

HYPERMOBILE ANKLES
bend back further than a ballet dancer's so they flap like flippers

Michael Phelps
After winning six golds in Athens, Michael, of Maryland, USA, won eight in Beijing, a total of fourteen ... more than any other Olympian ever! His body is perfect for swimming fast and not getting tired. As a child he was hyperactive but he's put all that activity to good use. In training, he eats 10,000 calories a day, five times more than an average man!

In 2004 the USA had led the gold medal table with thirty-six. China spent so much effort on training their athletes that in 2008 they topped the table with fifty-one. Among nine new events was Bicycle Motocross — BMX.

Two gold-winning Paralympians competed in the main games. Swimmer Natalie Du Toit of South Africa had lost her leg in a car accident. Table tennis player Natalya Partyka of Poland was born with no right arm.

LONDON

2012

At the spectacular opening ceremony a film showed James Bond escorting Queen Elizabeth II from Buckingham Palace to a helicopter which flew across London. Just as the film ended, a real helicopter arrived over the Olympic stadium from which Mr Bond and the Queen appeared to parachute . . .

FASTEST MAN EVER

Usain Bolt

Usain from Jamaica is the first sprinter to win six golds, three in both London and Beijing. He's been clocked at 28 miles an hour.

THE MOBOT

British athlete Mo Farah won gold in the 5,000 and the 10,000 metres. Everybody was soon copying his famous victory sign – the Mobot.

. . . and moments later the Queen came through the door of the royal box to open the games!

THREE TIMES OLYMPIC CITY – TWICE BY ACCIDENT!

An eruption of Mount Vesuvius brought the 1908 Games from Rome to London at the last minute. The Italian government needed to rebuild Naples and could no longer afford to hold them. In 1948 it was World War Two. With the world exhausted and two Olympiads missed, London stepped in. 2012 were the first Games that were planned to be in London . . . the only city to host them three times in the modern era.

RIO DE JANEIRO

2016

The first ever games to take place in South America. Events will be held all over this beautiful city.

THE MARACANÃ STADIUM

The Games will centre on this famous stadium. Originally built to host the 1950 FIFA World Cup, it was completely rebuilt for the 2014 World Cup.

BEACH VOLLEYBALL

THE 15TH PARALYMPICS

During the 1948 Olympics, a London hospital really started something when they held games for soldiers wounded in World War Two. 4,350 athletes will compete in the 15th Paralympics in Rio.

Although Beach Volleyball was invented in California, the first World Championships took place on Rio's Ipanema beach in 1987. It became an Olympic sport in 1996. Rio's 2016 arena will be on the equally famous Copacabana beach and is sure to be a highlight.

HOW THE GAMES HAVE GROWN

	1896 ATHENS	1936 BERLIN	1976 MONTREAL	2016 RIO
Athletes	245	3963	6084	10,500
Nations	14	49	92	206
Events	43	129	198	306
Most gold medals	USA (11)	Germany (33)	Soviet Union (49)	???

FASTER, HIGHER AND STRONGER?

Will the modern Olympics last a thousand years like the ancient Games ... or even longer?
Who knows what new sports, new traditions and new records the future may hold?

TOKYO

2020

Tokyo joins the select few cities to host the games for a second time. The National Stadium, where the opening and closing ceremonies for the 1964 Games were held, is being entirely rebuilt for the occasion.

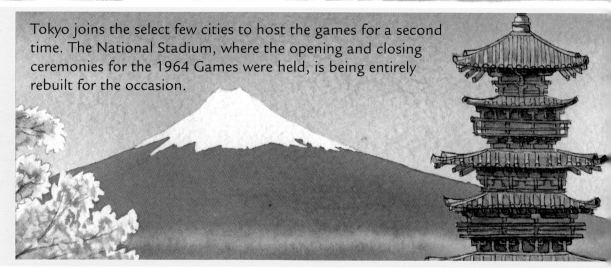

Depending where you're from, it may seem odd that baseball, cricket, rugby union or Basque pelota were once Olympic sports, or even odder that they no longer are.

Gliding was going to be included once but never was. Among others, competitors in American football, surf lifesaving and roller hockey would all like their sport included.

People constantly invent new sports. To qualify for the Olympics, sports mustn't rely on machines and enough countries need to take part.

Greece won most medals in the first modern Games. The USA have won most overall. Which nation will top the table in a hundred years' time?

In 2010, five thousand athletes aged between 14 and 18 took part in the first ever Youth Olympics in Singapore. IOC President Jacques Rogge said he was astonished by their Olympic spirit, which made the games the best ever. Baron Pierre would be proud of these champions of the future.